COMMUTING TIME

A Collection of Poems by

Geoffrey Davies

A.H. STOCKWELL
PUBLISHERS SINCE 1898

Published in 2023 by
Geoffrey Davies
in association with
Arthur H Stockwell Ltd
West Wing Studios
Unit 166, The Mall
Luton, Bedfordshire
ahstockwell.co.uk

British Library Cataloguing-in-Publication Data
A catalogue record for this book is available from the British Library.

ISBN: 9780722352915

Contents

Awake for the Living! 1
Backseat Driver. 2
Bells Ring Out 3
Commuting Time 4
Contra. 6
Daisy White and the Saga of Captain Black . . . 7
Dream On My Love 15
Dog Fight 16
Eleventh Heaven 18
Fishy Business 19
Friendship 20
Gun Dog 21
House Trading 22
Love 26
Mind Out!. 27
Naturally 28
Odour to Commuters 29
Passing Shadows 30
Requiem 31
Pride of the Tracks 32
Rich. 35
Saturday Night At the Movies 36
Sentiment or Logic? 39
Silver and Gold. 40
Silver Jubilation 42
The Alarm Cock 43
The Light Ahead 44
The Weather Cock 45
Togetherness 47
Vulcan QRA 48
Tomorrow Never Comes 50
When I'm Calling You 51

Introduction

I still find it hard to believe that in 1983, on a packed train of morning commuters travelling to work in London, somewhere between Ipswich and Colchester the train came to a grinding halt. As expected, the ticket inspector eventually arrived at our carriage and waved his hands for attention. We duly waited for his ritual delivery of apologies for overhead wires down, points failure or a trackside fire caused by an overloaded cable in the new signalling system... but not this time. Looking rather embarrassed, he gave the usual apology and announced the train had *run out of fuel!* Absolute silence followed as stunned passengers tried to adjust their minds to an unbelievable situation never experienced before. One could feel an angry tension building when, at this critical point, an American male voice broke the silence, "Gee! Thank God we're not flying!" – A humorous remark that reflected badly on us Brits. This incident actually happened and illustrates the level of stress that bombarded commuters' lives during the electrification of the main railway line between London Liverpool Street and Norwich. Seldom on time for work, stuck at signals or in sidings for hours at a time – commuters' prospects of staying employed were under constant threat.

In normal times, magazines and crossword puzzles are a pleasant distraction from the daily routine of travelling between home and work – however, these were not ordinary times. Short of a magic wand to dispel the ills of electrification, one needed a strong antidote to fight the anguish and despair plaguing passengers on the Eastern Region at this time.

However, it's strange how fate plays its hand. One evening I arrived back home to be greeted by my daughter with a poem she had written – homework from school that she wanted me to read and give an opinion. It had a nice imaginative flow and, as each stanza came under my scrutiny, I felt a surge of interest and excitement. I was impressed by what I read and thanked her, little knowing how her chance request would inspire me. Short stories and poetry were my strengths at school and probably influenced my position as sub-editor for the school magazine.

Here was the answer to my travelling nightmare – a window of opportunity to exercise old skills. *Commuting time,* for me, was about to be put to some useful purpose. With this in mind, I quickly acquired the necessary tools to embark on this new venture.

Each day railway commuters tend to use the same carriage and the same seat if possible; I followed suit and managed to establish my position next to a window. Pairs of passengers usually faced each other across a table and with writing materials to hand and two hard-backed books, I confronted the rigours of the journey. Both books had blank pages and lay open side-by-side and, for practical purposes, overlapped. This meant I could spread text over four pages, link ideas and experiment with words and situations without losing continuity.

Nearly always based on personal experience and observation, I have to say this book of poetry and verse evolved from a very untutored sorting house. You can imagine how enormously satisfying it was when characters and plot emerged fresh from the page and impacted favourably on the ears of interested travelling companions. They became my audience and sounding board; in fact, their responses enabled me to experiment with cause and effect. Laughter – or sometimes a tear – was evidence of the power of words and the extraordinary effect a slight nuance in a storyline can have on people's emotions. It was fun – and God only knows how many times I rewrote, altered and fine-tuned the results, always mindful that rhyming words, in my view, are only creditable if they hold meaning within the context of the subject; that alone was the crucial element that made it all work for me. My constraints were – and are – instinctive, dictated to a large extent by the movement and rhythm of the subject.

One morning curiosity got the better of me. A briefcase carrying the title 'Training Officer of the East Anglia Press Association' identified the fellow passenger sitting opposite – not one of my regulars. Anxious to get a professional view of my poetic enterprise, I confessed my opportunistic attempt to get his opinion. When finished he smiled and suggested I should publish but, in truth, I was writing for my own amusement and to save my sanity; publication, at that time was not an issue. However, in due course, the pandemic put pay to my musical hobby playing trumpet with the Bury St. Edmunds Concert Band; that closure revived my interest in poetry and narrative verse.

In conclusion, I dedicate this anthology to my wife and friend Elizabeth Ann and to my son Martin and daughter Christine who are the mainstay of our lives.

Geoff Davies

British Railways Eastern Region

AREA MANAGER,
LIVERPOOL STREET.

TO WHOM IT MAY CONCERN

y/r
o/r Date 8th August, 1986.

Dear Sirs,

This is to confirm that over recent weeks we have sufferred serious disruption to the train services into Liverpool Street from the Essex Area, because of major equipment failures and other serious incidents.

More specifically, yesterday we had multiple signal failures in the Stratford Area, and today a broken rail near Chelmsford, both resulting in delays of up to an hour and more on the journey into work.

May I apologise for the dreadful inconvenience this has caused.

The technical problems are under full investigation, as we are determined to take whatever practical steps are open to us to reduce their impact on our overall quality of service.

Yours faithfully,

C.M. HALL
AREA MANAGER

Eastern Region Railway Apology

Acknowledgements

Thank you to all my family, friends and professional associates who have encouraged me to pursue this poetic adventure.

I am indebted to Etienne de Villiers, past head of Walt Disney Europe; he kindly offered, through an associate, to promote my poetic enterprise.

I am amazed that Maurice Pooley, M.D. of Cell Film and Video Ltd made an animated film of the 'Alarm Cock' that had a second viewing at the Cannes Film Festival. Thank you Maurice, I still have a copy of the video and DVD.

Rob Head, much admired musical director of the Bury St. Edmunds Concert Band, premiered 'Saturday Night at the Movies' to a packed audience in the beautiful Theatre Royal at Bury St. Edmunds. It celebrated a concert of music using the same slogan.

Len Lawson and I were long serving members of the BSE Concert Band before COVID struck. Len is an author of several books and encouraged my poetic work. Thank you Band for sharing in my passion.

My heartfelt thanks for advice and help from Margaret Flowers, Pat Mitchell, Lewis Chapman, Chiron Richardson Todd, Mark Hamilton, Bob Bowman, Emily Gillings, Mirko and Tom Joyce, Secretary of the Farningham Old Boys Association.

In memoriam: Chief Technician Tam Kearns RAF, Crew Chief on board Mk2 Vulcan XJ824 on the day. A rare Scot with a great sense of humour and a good companion. Sadly, he died in the UK not long after the incident at Goose Bay, Labrador. See the footnote to the poem 'Vulcan QRA'.

In conclusion, my eternal thanks to Jim Hayes for producing a wonderful character reference on a farewell card which is proudly displayed at the end of this book.

Finally, my undying love and thanks to my family for putting up with me during long hours of deliberation.

Commuting Time

Welcome to my journey – an antidote for extreme delays and utter frustration; a book of poetry and verse aimed to amuse and entertain weary travellers. If you can read it, it's something you won't easily forget. The poems include *Daisy White and the Saga of Captain Black* about a pair of shire horses, *The Alarm Cock* which was made into an animated film and shown at the Cannes Film Festival, *Gun Dog, Saturday Night at the Movies* and many more. It's a collection of imaginative stories and memories that cover a lifetime.

Enjoy.

Awake for the Living!

Written: 23rd November 1986

Wake up to the freshness of spring's early days,
Frost-covered cobwebs, a filigree maze
The beauty of blossom beaconing bees
Awakening buds and new green leaves

Wake up to the sound of a church bell's ring,
Dawn's feathered chorus, songs on the wing,
The lap of a millpond, calm and serene,
Bubbling spring water, crystal and clean!

Wake up to the fragrance of hedgerows perfume,
Forget-me-nots, roses, violets in bloom,
Fennel and lavender, hops on the vine,
Wood smoke mingled with fresh-cut pine.

Wake up to the challenge of uncharted spaces,
Unknown, unconquered, adventurous places,
Unflinching brashness, the boldness of youth,
Rebelling at reason, defying the truth.

Wake up to the feeling, no worry or pain,
The absence of pressure, relief from all strain,
Freedom of minds! Please God, let it be!
United in peace, in a world that is free!

Backseat Driver

Written: November 1985

The sun was shining, a promising day,
Behind the wheel, on the Queen's highway,
A perfect day for a family treat,
But then came the voice from the car's back seat,

"You're driving too close! You're going too fast!
Look at that fool, too stupid to last,
No indications – engrossed in a chat.
There's no need for you to start acting like that!

The radio's loud, can't hear myself think,
Please close that window! Whew – what a stink!
Mind that lorry! It's a perfect disgrace,
There should be a net to hold that lot in place!

Look out he's braking! My God what a load,
It's going to avalanche into the road!
Quick put your foot down, for goodness' sake,
There's plenty of room – go on overtake!

Hang on a minute! My word you're a clot,
Should I always remind you when you have forgot?
You missed the last turn off! When can I depend?
You're enough to drive anyone right round the bend!"
"Yes Dear."

Bells Ring Out

Written: 15th June 1988

Bells ring out, the pipes are playing,
Radiant beauty all around.
Amidst God's flowers, joined together,
Each to each your lives are bound,

And may this love you share together,
And the vows that you have sworn,
Grow and strengthen as time passes.
Beyond the sound of Gabriel's horn.

Commuting Time

Written: December 1983

Commuting by train, was a strain on the brain,
Timekeeping schedules were cruel,
Hours wasted when points seized up in their joints,
And diesels ran out of fuel.

Just once in a while, commuters would smile,
Punctuality reigned and 'twas fine,
But the gloom soon came back when they learnt that the track,
Had overhead wires on the line.

'Now don't you fuss, we've laid on a bus,
From Witham to Colchester Town.
Don't raise your voice, we give you a choice.'
'Yes, but Stowmarket is where we get down!'

'Sir, it's a shame, but I tell you again,
Twenty minutes will soon put it right.'
But two hours from now, there's a hell of a row,
And it seems that we're stuck for the night.

'Contingency planning, does that include manning,
To fix up the wires over head?'
'Yes, sir it does, but we've just had a buzz!
They're apparently all home in bed!'

In the gloom of the night, it seemed that a fight,
Was about to break out in the crowd,
In the midst of this scene, the signals turned green,
'All aboard,' someone shouted out loud!

At last, we're in luck, thank God we're not stuck,
Better hurry, the driver's got in,
With no more ado we stand in the queue,
At the buffet car bar for our sin.

The barman stood there, too tired to care,
'I've been up since five this morning,'
It wasn't a lie, he looked fit to die,
His mouth stretched, continually yawning!

At the bar of the diner, you could hear one hard liner,
Whose last round had lapsed into eight,
'My wife'll have a fit.'
'Don't give me that bit.
Have another before it's too late.'

With a lurch we were off, too thankful to scoff,
How easy our lives turn to grief,
With gathering speed our nightmare was freed.
Progress at last, and relief.

The mellowing brew took its toll of the few,
Content with a paralysed brain,
For them just as well, now devoid of the hell,
From more hours cooped up in the train.

As if by design, we were stopped down the line,
With others to front and to rear,
One man from Marks Tey, had bent down to pray,
Frustration had shed its last tear.

One gent who knew better, was composing a letter,
This chaos was bending his mind,
As day followed night, there was no end in sight.
And complaining was one endless grind!

By sweat of the brow, eventually Stow,
Looms out from the blackness of night,
But, one consolation, the staff at the station,
Apologised much at our plight!

Remember the letter? It made him feel better,
A reply and free ticket were sent,
But on the day and the date, he was two hours late,
His patience was finally spent.
Without further fuss he took to the bus!

Contra

Written: May 1983

The bareness of truth, one must agree,
Is only skin deep in its nudity,
Untruth is a cover up, that slopes under test,
Lies beneath the surface, poised to cause unrest.

Daisy White and the Saga of Captain Black

Written: June 1989

This is the story of a pair of Shire horses I knew as a boy, they both worked on a farm belonging to the Famingham Homes for Little Boys at South Darenth near Dartford in Kent – my home for nine years between 1943 and 1952. 'Spud picking', a slang expression for harvesting potatoes, was an annual event of self-sufficiency, helping to feed upwards of three hundred boys, many the victims of the war. George was an 'Old Boy' who stayed on at the farm after serving a Farming Apprenticeship at the 'Homes'.

"Come on Daisy, stir yourself, an early start today!
The cock has crowed and boots approach, we'll soon be on our way,"
"Sorry, Captain. Something's wrong, not feeling very bright!"
Captain's head bent down to see the reason for my plight.
Seconds later master George flung wide the stable door,
Dawn's grey light cast shadows on the cobbled, straw strewn, floor.

"Well, there you are my beauties, time to start the day!"
With clicking tongue – "Come on you two, the manger's full of hay!"
Fetlocks brushed, plaited manes, Dubbin on each trace,
Shoes strike stones, a shower of sparks, as bits are put in place.
"Whoa, there boy! I'll tighten girth – and don't you hold or cough!"
With clopping hooves, we follow George out to the water trough.

"Captain!" "Well, what is it girl?" "I hope you're feeling strong!"
"What's up my girl, still got that pain? the first job won't take long,
It's easy work, we're spinning spuds, it should be rather fun!
Remember last year's battlefield, potatoes by the ton?"
"Ah yes, it was embarrassing, poor George pulled out his hair!
Those boys from school broke every rule, potatoes everywhere."
"Gee up there, we've not much time, it's getting pretty late!"
In single file we follow George out through the farmyard gate.
"Whoa there, steady Daisy!" George reached and placed his sack,
Closed the gate and, in one leap, sat sideways on my back.

An ambling gait by gravelled lane, hedgerows late in bloom,
A heady way to start the day in nature's rich perfume.
The path we tread un-metalled now, a track of velvet green,
A tree-lined verge along one side provides an orchard screen.
Many a time hitched to the cart, we've trod this leafy route.
Back at sundown to our boys, the cart full up with fruit!

Warming sun, shrinking mist, cobwebs silver thread,
With swishing tails, we onward plod with Captain up ahead,
"Don't worry Daisy, nearly there, a fairly level field!"
Serene and green and there it was, our patch of Kentish Weald.
Tightening harness, spinners bite, each tine unearths its prize,
Reds and whites amongst the clods for searching hands and eyes.
An hour elapsed of steady toil, the pain I felt still there.
Then in the distance, faint at first, excitement filled the air!

Chattering, laughter, names were called, and bodies soon appear,
Growing larger, two by two, they jump and skip and cheer!
"Hello Daisy! Captain! George!" Surrounded now, we stop.
"Right then boys there's work to do, there's quite a tidy crop!"
A little lad looked up at me. "Come Daisy, let's be friends."
Then George cried out! "Don't feed 'em spuds,
it makes 'em cough both ends."
Laughter rippled through the ranks, awareness on their faces.
Then the tedious marking out, two boys each twenty paces.

The day wore on, the sun was high, the boys were working well,
Occasionally a scuffle broke that George was quick to quell,
Lunchtime came, and off they went, an hour passed or more.
A cart was hitched and loads of spuds were clamped in earth and straw.
We had our nosebags and some hay, while George had forty winks,
Exhausted trying to keep the peace, tired out by boys' hijinks!
But not for long before the throng, came back to join the fray.
Encouraged by a morning's work and labouring for pay!

"Captain! I feel weak and sick and, throbbing in my head,"
"It's probably the spuds you ate, you know what George has said?"
"I'm sure you're wrong, my jet-black shire, but never mind we'll see,
If what you did last autumn-time has this effect on me!"
A boy cried out! "Just look at that! Just look at Captains thing!"
Amazed they stood and stared agog – then came the fateful sting!

Eyes turned wild, and nostrils flared, a raging whinnying cry,
Legs and body flexed and strained, hooves flayed and pawed the sky!
"Whoa there!" But to no avail, he bucked and snatched the traces,
Tore his halter, snapped the stays, girth straps, reigns, and braces.
With flying tail and fluttering mane, he raced off in a breeze,
Scattering boys, crashed through a hedge towards some distant trees.

George unhitched me. "Come on boys – don't stand there, clear the way!
Now then Daisy, do your best, there's no time for delay!"
George was flustered, all confused, control was out of hand,
Boys had gathered into groups, a battle had been planned.
A cheer went up, and fights broke out; George jabbed me in the rump,
Flying spuds were every-where I started with a jump.
Too late, the force with which I moved, unseated George from me,
The boys thought this was super fun and clapped their hands with glee!

Not heeding words, I galloped off, my efforts turned to pain,
I couldn't stop; for Captains sake I had to bear the strain.
Through a hedge, some broken wires, trees, a stream's dry bed,
Hoof prints stopped and then I saw, I thought that he was dead!
A bundled heap, a bulbous mound, entangled in a briar,
My heart sank low, I slowly walked towards my special shire.
"Captain! Captain! Speak to me! Just tell me you're alright!"
Steam rose gently where he lay. I froze there, sick with fright!

A puttering throb pricked up my ears, the sound distinct and clear,
Growing louder as it came. I whinnied out of fear.
And then I saw the iron horse, it stopped, and George appeared.
He limped and hobbled, then he saw, and tears coursed through his beard,
"Heavens above, what have we here. My God what have we done?
What made you do it Captain boy, what made you up and run?"
Captain moved at George's voice." Oh Lord you've cuts and scores,"
The voice infused that 'mighty heart' to heave up on all fours,
Barbed wire wrapped around his girth, cut deep into his hide,
A pool of blood was evident, where he lay on his side.

With caution, George approached his 'pride' without another sound,
Then, at his touch poor Captain crashed, and pinned George to the ground.
A cry for help! A whinnying snort! I cantered round about.
Two boys emerged from Iron Horse, but George had now passed out.
One was Roy the other Pete, they both helped on the farm,
"Alright Roy, I'll stay with George; you go and raise alarm!
Take the tractor, and make haste, but first go get the rope,
I'll do my best to get George free I think that I can cope!

With wary strides, and soothing words. "Come Daisy, you know Pete?"
You're all I've got, and this 'ere rope to free our Georges feet."
Concern and anguish on Pete's face, an arm wiped sweating brow,
He quickly tied the rope round me, then over hanging bough,
The coiled-up end hurled in an arc, unwinding as it flew,
The hard whipped end down with a thud, amid the sickly view,
No time for gazing or despair, Pete's hands were deft and quick,
In one movement grabbed the rope and breaking off a stick,
Started pumping soft brown earth, as busy as a mole,
Tunnelled under Captains legs, enough to make a hole.
The rope thread through, legs bound and tied, Pete worked on tirelessly,
"OK, Daisy! Easy now! That's it! We've got them free!"

George looked awful, pale and drawn, then briefly blinked an eye,
And as we lowered Captain's legs – I thought I heard a sigh!
A sign of hope, I nudged his nose, then snorted in his ear,
I jumped back startled when he moved, then faintly, "Daisy, dear,
Oh, Daisy! Daisy! Is it you? Where am I? Ah, the pain!"
Neck veins bulged he raised his head, then, passed out once again.

A chilling air of silence hung 'round us like a cloak,
Attention now to Roy's return, as breathlessly he spoke,
"The ambulance can't get here and the tractor's broken down,
We need to reach the viaduct and the road to Dartford town,
You're best with Daisy, Peter! I'll help you on your way,
We'll get George onto Daisy's back, and then I'd better stay.
Now, it's up to you and Daisy, to get George to that road,
The ambulance crew will meet you there and help transfer your load!"

Chalky boulders, scattered flints that shattered under foot.
Gorse and bramble, clinging vine, the odd protruding root,
Balmy darkness into light, a sudden sharp report!
Clapping wings, a hundred-fold, smack out their loud retort!
A fearful impulse made me start – Pete hauled me back in check,
"Steady Daisy, that's my girl." He reached and stroked my neck.
On we trudged through nettle beds, I couldn't clear my mind,
Anxious thoughts of Captains fate; the mess we'd left behind.

Groans from George and echoed shouts, the chuffing of a train,
Eclipsed by phantom galloping hooves pummelling my brain.
Everything a misty dream whispering voices, gone.
Sinking down to emptiness, complete oblivion!
Emerging voices, urgent pleas. "Come on, we can't lose you!
Oh Daisy, thank the lord you're here, thank
God we've pulled you through!"
Excitement hung on every word! What did they have to say?
Light and darkness flicked and merged awareness died away.

Conscious now, a guttering light flounced shadows on the floor
Out of nowhere, flooding pain like none I've felt before,
I tried to rise – to no avail – a stab whipped through my frame.
"Come on boys, I need the soap, and please adjust that flame!
We've work to do and little time." He faltered in his speech,
"It seems to me, from what I feel, she's going to have a breech!"
Involuntary spasms came, my head began to spin,
My mind's eye focussed on the spot, where hands groped deep within.
Excruciating pain ensued, constriction in my throat,
Vision dimmed, the pain intense, surroundings seemed remote.
"Oh look! Oh look!" I heard them cry. the
vet's voice soothed. "There, there."
One little lad with mouth agape could only stand and stare.
The little lad, now out of shock, tears tumbling down his face!
Clapped his hands as others sounds, began to fill the place.
The vet's voice boomed! "Now – quiet lads – this day's been quite a test,
Daisy has her lovely foal and now she needs her rest."

The hollow ring of voices faded, echoed echoes, fainter still,
Through the night to dawns awakening, whistle from the paper mill.

A towering chimney dwarfs the archways –
white plumes rise above the stack.
Nearby river ripples silver, turns from slate grey into black,
Dances out in morning sunlight, rapidly it chatters on,
Froths and foams past roads and houses in its effort to be gone.
Gentle chimes drift down the valley from the chapel on the hill,
Sunshine spreads its glowing mantle, warmth disturbs the morning chill.

Robin red breast, lark and linnet, thrush and blackbird, tit and wren,
Flit and twitter, flute their hearts out, farmyard cocks crow now and then,
Snapping twigs, a rustling snuffling prickly spines and pinpoint eyes,
Snout aquiver, pauses, scratches, and then I saw to my surprise!
Black as midnight, eyes a twinkling, came and searched for natures store,
Another Captain in the making, born within these walls of straw.
Horsebox, tractor, trailer, people; – chattering voices amplified!
Roy and Pete were first to reach us, ropes, were speedily untied,

Disappearing bales and fencing, null the trauma of the night,
Through the tumult Roy was saying "What about the name Starlight!"
"Sir!" Pete's voice was now appealing. "May we give the colt a name?"
"Sorry Pete, I wish you could; but in good faith George has that claim!"
Then. "Starlight it is!" A voice familiar, carried from the crowd behind,
"A lovely name you'll all be proud of, and two more things I have in mind,"
George was sitting in a wheelchair, two black boxes on a tray
"Roy and Pete, a small momentum; because of you I live today."
But choked with sorrow, grief, and sadness, whispered,
"Captain Black has passed away!"

Farningham Home for Boys 1864–1961

Photo by courtesy of London News Agency Photos Ltd.

No Blind Alley for Farningham Boys!

OUR MOTTO IS:

From Misfortune through Happy Boy-hood to Responsible Manhood at The Homes for Boys, Farningham.

FIELD-MARSHAL THE VISCOUNT MONTGOMERY on his visit to the Homes in August, 1945, said: "We have won the War, and we have to win the Peace. . . . This job has got to be taken over by the Youth of the Nation. . . . It is for lads such as you to take up the running with enthusiasm."

Will you please help to keep one of these boys at Farningham ?

President of the Farningham Boys Homes, Field Marshal Montgomery, states his plea and vision of the boy's usefulness to society (1945)

'Monty' and the boys

SOMETHING DOING

Every opportunity is given for practical knowledge of agriculture, and scores of our old boys are doing well as farmers, not only in their own country, but in Canada, Australia, &c.

The Bakers lead a very busy life, for in their shop the daily needs of both Farningham

Farmers

and Swanley are supplied. Under the control of a thoroughly skilled baker and confectioner, the boys are taught the making and baking of bread, cakes, etc., and the business of a pastrycook. The department offers the greatest facilities for acquiring a complete knowledge of the trade, whilst the quality and wholesomeness of its products are of the best, as evidenced by the commendation passed by expert, and the high standard of excellent maintained in the general health of the boys.

Extract from a 50-year souvenir publication of the Boys Home unique story, with no mention of the First World War (1914)

Dream On My Love

Written: April 2007

The ghosts that haunt our memories are never real it seems,
Just vague illusions from our past, that taunt us in our dreams,
But come what may the light of day, confirms my point of view.
The best dream in reality is sharing life with you!

Dog Fight

Written: March 1983

- *1936: Bom Kings College Hospital London.*
- *1940: Partially blinded by a stray cat during the Blitz of London.*
- *1941/43: Moved to Northampton. Mother deserted our family home.*
- *1943: Placed in the Famingham Homes for Little Boys*

On track for London, the V1 Flying Bombs posed a threat to the 'Homes'. 'Dog fights' high in the sky were an exciting spectable each day for three hundred boys. We boys were subsequently evacuated directly by rail to Taunton in Somerset.

Hands thrust deep in pockets, bracers stretching down,
From narrow shoulders, red check shirt, short trousers limp and brown.
Thick-soled boots, black and bright, laced up with leather thong.
A homeless mite, who's family life a war had deemed to wrong.

Spindly legs, freckled face, long fair curly hair,
Face up-turned, neck stretched out in concentrated stare.
In silence high above his head, excitement filled his glance,
The distant specs that caught his eye transfixed him in a trance.

Darting in and of clouds, like minnows in a brook,
Silver objects flew and hid, as others sought to book!
Seeking out friend from foe, by ident, marks and figures,
Crosses, roundels, swastikas; as fingers twitched on triggers.

Shimmering haze over yellow gorse, a rustling, gentle breeze,
Brushing purple clover fields, stirring through the trees.
Trilling larks arise in song, and flutter in the air,
Exulting to the countryside, so pleasant, green and fair.

The hum of busy worker bees suddenly, silenced by the drone,
Of a hundred pulsing engines that, labour, throb and groan,
Carrying their excess weight of an evil lethal load,
To homesteads, towns, and villages, to drop, erupt, explode!

Spitfires wheeling high above in skies of azure blue,
Contrails even higher, spreading fans of paler hue,
Puffs of red, thick, black, smoke, swirl and blot the sun
As cannon and machine-gun fire wreak havoc with the Hun.

Escorting fighters join the fray, some ME109's,
They pit their wits, to stop the Spit's breaking up their lines.
Relentlessly the carnage spreads, as shadows start to loom,
O'er harvest fields, where broken shields,
have crashed and met their doom.

A Golden Orb in coral skies, salutes the ending day,
With luminescent violet beams edged with silver grey.
Against this jewelled backdrop are flashing glints of light,
As hunters speed in hot pursuit to blast the foe from sight.

Supermarine Spitfire

Eleventh Heaven

Written: December 1990

Eleven years we've been together,
Eleven years of toil and bliss!
Eleven years of trial and error,
Eleven years to come to this,
Eleven years to make our minds up,
Eleven years to all come true.
Eleven years to tie the knot,
Eleven years to say, I do!

Fishy Business

Written: Jaunary 1985

We swim and we play in our pond every day,
We are fish with a fixed point of view,
We don't look for trouble, when the occasional bubble,
Is burst by one of our few.

In a safe frame of mind no looking behind,
No fear of the net or the hook,
Our waters are calm, no cause for alarm,
Just the rippling feed from a brook.

We share our ability, our sea is tranquillity,
Not hooked on a strong party line,
We don't need to vote, our don't knows can't float,
No Black Rod to tackle our shrine.

But the truth of our fate concerns matters of state,
Where rough seas and tempests prevail,
Where the harpoon and gun are fisherman's fun,
And each wave has a whip in its tail.

So whatever we wish, we become processed fish,
Not gutted and cleaned as of old,
With psychological pills we are stuffed to the gills,
To prevent a political cold.

Friendship

Written: January 1987

How strange our friendships, people meet,
In the twinkling of an eye, we know and like the people that we greet.
Time is no barrier, a pendant still,
Locked in space, silent, a passage blocked that bears no ill.
It floats above the morass of life's inferno!
Intact, impervious to the unpredictable, until it's time to go.
P.S. But with regrets, should we not meet again.

Gun Dog

Written: April 1986

I have the waggiest stump of tail, I'm liver brown and white,
My ears are long, and when I run my eyes flap out of sight,
I'm a little springer spaniel, and Hector is my name,
I spend most days beside the fire and dream I'm chasing game!

The most important thing I've got well, not when in repose,
Is the large brown lump above my teeth – my double-barrelled nose!
I'm taken walkies daily, with my mistress by my side,
I come to heel when it suits me, then match her stride for stride.

The other day was different though, with master and the boys,
In the orchard shooting apples to get me used to noise,
The grass was high, I jumped and sprang, my efforts aimed to please,
Doing all those sniffing bits and watering the trees!

"Now come on son, take up that gun, grip firm but not too tight,"
Before I knew, the gun went off! And so did I, with fright!
I tore off through the thicket with the blast still in my ears,
My tail end scorched and burning; my eyes a flood of tears.

Straight home I went, and in full cry, a bullet through the grass,
Escaping from the maniac who shot me in the Ah-hmm!
My sympathetic mistress, both practical and kind,
Trussed me up to extricate the lead from my behind!

Stung into reaction at the start of my ordeal
With lightning speed my parts were plugged as lead was met by steel
"Your bot is like a pepper pot!" Her knee thrust in my ear,
"But to succeed, I think you'll need an armour-plated rear".

I heard my master and the boys, as they approached the door,
In they came, and laid the blame, excuses by the score.
In one respect they were correct, with that I must agree.
My downfall largely was because I peed and missed the tree!

House Trading

(A Very Moving Experience)

Written: December 1985

Whenever it seems, that the house of our dreams,
Falls within our financial bracket,
We hardly begin when frustration sets in,
We get caught in the house-trading racket.

When we want to buy, we have to rely,
On a system where price has no ceiling,
To buy we must sell, which adds to the hell,
We are trapped and are now double-dealing.

Our selected estate, has a board at the gate,
'For Sale,' and a number to call,
We ring and are told, it is probably sold,
And they can't raise the vendor at all.

Several days later, we see in the paper,
The properties still up for sale,
The agent is free, so we view and agree,
With some effort we're sure we can't fail.

Before sale agreed, a mortgage we need,
And probably more, for repairs,
A new heating installation, to boost the equation
With rates and travelling fares.

The house is surveyed the surveyor is paid,
And may be, again, and again!
Each new contender is blind to the vendor,
Who loses, and who stands to gain?

The building society with restraint and sobriety,
Consider the pros of our case,
First, the mortgage is on, then they think it's a con.
The house has a crack in its base!

The property's old, and so we are told,
To get estimates for all the repairs,
But doubts have been sown, and advancing a loan,
Will not serve our interests or theirs.

An exploratory bore, right under the floor,
Should show the extent of the crack,
And with new drains in the ground, for X number of pounds,
Subsidence should never come back!

With surveyor and builder, it begins to bewilder,
More thorns in the deeds to this plot,
Woodworm in the doors, dry rot in the floors,
Our Pakenham paradise shot!

It's getting us down, we're beginning to frown,
We have nothing to cheer or make merry!
It's becoming a pain, more cash down the drain,
Ah well! Back to the agents in Bury.

A perpetual strain, we are part of a chain,
Each link a potential flaw,
No anchor or stay, total freedom of play,
No confines or governing laws.

The estate agent chap has a large folded map,
With pockets and bumph, by the reams,
We set off with a smile, that fades with each mile,
Like glamour, it's not what it seems.

Each leaflet has views, which should give us clues,
But many seem tricks to deceive,
A view from the side takes us all for a ride,
Not detached as we're led to believe.

Hour after hour in the valley of Stour.
Bures looks a promising place,
A barn conversion, is a major diversion,
But the price puts us out of that race.

"Now then my dear, it's no use, I fear!
Let's try nearer home once again,
Last night from my pillow, I saw Walsham-le-Willows,
Has a house, in a quiet country lane.

Let's hope fate is kind, what a fortunate find,
Full of grace and Edwardian charm,
The garden is grand, with room to expand,
Not far from the village or farm!"

Our plans were laid and arrangements were made,
The vender was happy to wait,
But events were to prove, when ready to move,
How a solicitor altered our fate.

Ours was a gem; he tried to get them,
To honour agreements of sale,
But the vendor was dumb, content to succumb,
And our pleas were of little avail.

Whatever we choose, we are destined to lose,
You'd think it was time to give in,
All dispensation, no compensation,
Lost fortunes before we begin,

From Layer-de-le-Haye, to remote Hinderclay,
Via Rickenhall, Botesdale and Diss,
Visits to Thurston, and Woolpit, and Drinkstone,
Selection was now hit or miss!

The saying you've heard, concerning a bird,
In the hand is worth two in a bush,
Friends with that name, had been watching our game,
And decided to give us a push!

"Why not try Bardwell? It's a nice place to dwell,
There's a house we think you should see."
"It's not very far, just minutes by car."
Days later we view and agree!

The house looked nice and so was the price,
The landlord was eager to sell,
But before we could buy, we had to comply,
And deal with the agents as well.

It's useless to plead, it didn't succeed,
When ethics and patience are tried,
No court of appeal, would ever reveal,
What an agent had managed to hide.

It's hard to believe, or even conceive,
Our intentions were ever in doubt,
It seemed so untrue, like a bolt from the blue,
Our buyers were now opting out!

It made our hearts bleed, one more sale agreed,
Almost lost in this crazy affair,
To our utter dismay the very next day,
Our vendors were selling elsewhere.

By sweat blood and tears, you age several years,
You perceive that this practice is rife,
You part with your health and a large chunk of wealth,
The biggest investment in life.

With violence in view, we threaten to sue,
There's no honour to winning this game,
No bishop or knight, to aid in this plight,
And no one to shoulder the blame!

Well! You weave and you duck, and eventually luck,
Plays its part, in satirical fashion.
With diminishing pain, you breath once again,
You forget all the heat and the passion.

Thank God we have views, and the freedom to choose,
But what travesties of justice and laws?
And the promises lost, to our ultimate cost,
Confused in the 'whys, ways and wherefores?

Love

Written: April 1986

I wish it were easy to understand love,
What causes this natural attraction?
Emotional poles, often miles apart,
Incensed to the point of distraction.

Mother to father to baby is one,
That isn't a mystery to solve,
Providing that love and not lust, was the drive,
Behind their parental resolve!

In grammar, both abstract and proper,
You come to a verb's adjectival conclusion,
Its objective, descriptive, most active permissive,
Which add to the total confusion

So, what do we mean when we say 'I love you,
I love it, it was love at first sight.'
It's possessive, protective, in some ways aggressive,
But blind? I doubt that is right – but it is confusion!

Mind Out!

Written: 1985

Hopelessly they stand and stare,
Minds seem blank and unaware,
Tell me! Do you really care?
Then fight to liberate the snare,
Of souls trapped between somewhere,
And normality, balanced by a hair,
That thread of hope we see out there,
As science and technology declare
Genetic research advancing stem cells year on year,
Support we need, this common ground to share,
For special needs, and special deeds, new methods to prepare
With drugs and notes observing violence, another broken chair,
Head banging, self-mutilation, causes for despair,
Yet different! Their ecstasy unreal – unable to compare,
The pain enjoyed from punching, pulling hair!
Expended to exhaustion, while minding helpers swear,
To find an answer – an answer to a prayer,
That with Gods help and ours, we'll find that key so rare,
To unlock, unscramble, restructure, tie up loose ends, repair,
Instinctive traits, emotions, abstract elements, fear.
Do not be mindless of this case make everyone aware!
Responsibility is for everyone to share,
The cost, the capitol of our cross to bear!

Naturally

Written: 1980

The flight of a swallow, the song of a thrush,
A fond embrace, a sigh, then hush,
A strand of hair caught on a summer breeze,
Hand in hand under shady green trees.

Whispering leaves, the sun without haste,
Entwining fingers, a hand 'round the waist,
Twinkling eyes looking up from the ground,
Spring and summer their nectar abound.

The moon up above, flock mountains a kiss,
A caress, a murmur, a touch of the lips.
Finger tips lingering o'er pallid sheen.
Tender the night over lover's calm scene.

A gentle reproach, a whimper, a cry,
A thrust of passion that reaches high,
Raising the threshold of nature's intent,
The climax, the gasp, the final content.

Odour to Commuters

Written: 1983

In a roundabout way, it's hard to say,
A commuter's life is much fun.
They're up at dawn, all shaven and shorn,
To catch a train on the run.

From their beds and lost sleep they are herded like sheep,
Into carriages, tubes and buses,
Squashed like sardines, with the day's magazines,
Enfolding and binding like trusses.

All breathless and bland, there's magic wand,
To dispel the dawns deep depression,
It starts once again, when they miss the last train,
Or 'twas cancelled, without rhyme or reason.

At the end of the day, the money they pay,
For travel, is far from belief,
They take a hard bash, yet lay out their cash,
For the taxman who gives no relief!

Passing Shadows

Written: August 1986

As the first rays pierce the skies,
Nocturnal creatures hide their eyes,
Passing shadows turn to grey,
As other creatures greet the day,

Lapwings, soar and turn and twist,
Swoop and dive through swirling mist,
By wooded copse and leafy spires,
Dawn's awakening feathered choirs,

Unsettled now, the sun breaks through,
Arrow shafts strike pearly dew,
Tiny rainbows light each drop,
Diamond glints on lace-strewn crop,

Chill air stirred by thermal breeze,
Shimmering light through dancing leaves,
Gently swaying timber towers,
Shadow puffs, from needle bowers,

Disappearing shades of night,
Trees awake to changing light,
Bustling, bristling, upturned spears,
Pipe their fluted, arias.

The stage is set, another play,
Begins at dawn on each new day!

Requiem

(Farewell to Innocence)

Written: October 1998

Fill up your cup, throw off dull care,
Wrap up those feelings of despair,
Death's door flung wide, accepts a life has passed
From life to life through pearly gates, a life that lasts
and lasts.

Loved one's are there await you to come in.
Where life after life is peace and joy only found within.
And as you go rejoicing, we join in what they say,
"God and His Angels welcome you to Paradise this day."

Pride of the Tracks

(The Duchess of Hamilton)

Written: April 1984

This poem was inspired by the beauty and grace of the immaculately-streamlined steam locomotive The Duchess of Hamilton. Along with the fastest steam locomotive in the world 'Mallard', the Duchess is on static display at the National Railway Museum, York.

The Duchess of Hamilton

In her mantle of red, streamlined with gold,
Gleaming she stands, impatient and bold,
Primed and pressured with vaporous power,
This Duchess is ready to leave on the hour!

Porters assisting with passengers' cases,
Observing farewells with resolute faces,
Loud speakers bark; porters withdraw,
Echoes die from the last slammed door,

Twin horns trump, smoke blooms from her stack,
Safety valves vent, hissing steam on the track,
The guard's whistle shrills; a green flag is showing!
Precise on the hour! It's time to be going!

A thunderous blast, the spinning wheel,
The visible lurch of a mountain of steel,
Exploding black columns with red topped plumes,
Carboniferous belches and sulphurous fumes,

Gathers momentum, rails take the strain,
Sleepers awake to the oncoming train.
Leaving the station and out on the line,
Smoke fills the space where the sun used to shine.

Pistons and wheels an invisible blur,
Landscapes unfold and occupants stir,
In pastures and fields with daisies and thistle,
Cattle look up to the sound of her whistle,

Some bolt away kicking clods in the air,
Others chew cud with a stupefied stare,
A blanket – a shroud – a black and white screen,
Spreads over pastures both luscious and green,

As fast as a bullet she speeds through the grass,
On lines straight as arrows and polished like glass.
White clouds of vapour that stream from her funnel,
Are soon swallowed up as she enters a tunnel.

Silence once more from the clatter and clack,
As the guards' van at last disappears from the track,
The smell lingers on long after the sight,
Of the Duchess in motion, powering past in full flight!

Mallard, the fastest steam locomotive in the world

Rich

Written: March 1984

I woke this morning, my world seemed so grey,
I can't understand why it varies each day?
Like a hurricane's breath, sudden winds of despair,
Yet, by yesterday's contrast, I hadn't a care!

How often I've wished when I'm feeling blue,
To brush back those clouds for the sun to shine through,
But whatever you do to alter this trend,
It's stupid to think this pattern will end.

Rest assured, it is true, life is balanced that way,
God never intended the same every day!

Saturday Night At the Movies

(The Palace of Dreams)

Written: January 1982

Dedicated to Rob Head MD and all members of the Bury St. Edmunds Concert Band, this poem was premiered at the Theatre Royal Bury St. Edmunds on 15th February 2014. It was narrated by Rob as an introduction to the concert 'Saturday Night At the Movies'.

Dark winter evenings, stood two by two,
Waiting for hours, pairs in a queue.
Blustering drizzle, can't wait to go in,
A shape in the gutter creating a din,
Scraping a tune from bow and bent saw,
An ear to the ground, and an eye for the law.
A dog joins in with a howling lament,
Throat to the sky, scruffy – unkempt!
The Palace awakes, faces aglow,
The Commissionaire barks. "We're ready to go!
Let's keep it moving! We ain't got all night!"
A shock to the system, the queue jumps with fright

The ropes are removed, the doors are flung wide,
Legs become fluid, swept in on a tide!
'No pushing or shoving! Come on, play the game,
There's plenty of seats, they're all priced the same!'
People, lunge forward, one makes a fuss,
Drenched to the skin by the splash from a bus.
But all that's forgotten, once through the doors,
Mock marble columns, plush carpet floors.
Gold buttons, red jacket, pass by in a flash,
Machines pumping tickets, tinkling cash,
Lighting reflects and refracts a green glow,
With letters and arrows that show where to go.
Potted palms for the circle, nymphs on the walls,
Red curtains and flowers for those in the stalls.

The main film's still showing, a few minutes late,
A ticket attendant instructs us to wait.
'Don't be impatient, I saw it last night,
The first one gets rough and ends in a fight!'
We sit in the foyer with its huge chandelier,
Muffled music drifts in, an occasional cheer.
Portraits look down with their glowing appeal,
Eyes become dazzled, it doesn't seem real.
Abruptly it thunders, then quietens down,
Up-stood for the Anthem, respect for the crown.
Usherettes with bright faces appear on the scene,
Red costumes and lipstick, perfume, pure sheen!
The Palace is emptied out on to the streets,
As we are invited to take up our seats.

Like Royals we enter a vast palatial hall,
So high, the Gods allow some to sit tall.
Row upon row and tier upon tier,
The seats spread a fan from the front to the rear.
Crimson, silver, a clocks golden face,
Amber globes suspended like moons hung in space!
Lights are dimmed down as we reach our row,
'Please be careful! Mind how you go!
Pull yourselves in, it's a bit of a squeeze,
Flip up the seats, they swing back from the knees!"

A torch probes the darkness, exploring each place,
In the semi lit gloom, its beam throws a trace!
Foot lights and spot lights, yellow and blue,
The acre sized curtains reflecting their hue,
Bright flashing faces as matches are lit,
The organ ascends from the orchestra pit,
The mighty Wurlitzer's pipes shake with sound,
Vibration, enough to lift seats from the ground.
One spot shines on the organist's head,
Reflecting his grin and a faint glimpse of red,
Carnation buttonhole and twinkling feet,
Peddles, push stops, a rotating seat.
'Good evening, all!' A trump on the keys,
'A few tunes, a song, so join in do please!'
With mellowing warmth, we soon settle back,
The organ descends; surroundings are black,

Fanfares! A cockerel! The curtains then part,
Exposing the screen, the news for a start.
The décor offsets the black and the white,
The main feature's coloured, real blood in a fight,
Well – real it seems, and blows that are struck,
Cause even the hardest to flinch and to duck,
And when men are thrown, it isn't a stunt,
Not to us anyway – with a sympathised grunt!
Intermission steps in with a strong focussed beam,
Radiating her wares of sweets and ice cream,
The news, two features, three hours of bliss,
At the back of the stalls, the odd stolen kiss,
From 'Chaplin' to 'The Killing Fields', laughter and screams,
Transported away on a carpet of dreams.
The anthem, the end, the cycle complete,
Reality bites, and it's back to the street!

Sentiment or Logic?

Written: December 1986

Now listen my friends, it's us that they tell,
Life is so precious, and war is hell
An eye for an eye, no hanging no more,
No life for a life, when we're breaking the law?
What sense does it make? Crime figures increase!
Yet nuclear death holds a nuclear peace.
Contradiction of terms – what's murder about?
Deterrents are used to remove any doubt,
That would be transgressors ignoring convention,
Take heed of results, too horrific to mention,
The fear of destruction brought peace and respect,
So why is it that hanging's no longer correct?
To deter any thoughts of murder and rape,
And the criminal mind, no way of escape!
The logic of war seems to work on one hand,
So why not reverse the law of the land?
Bring hanging back, for a short while at least,
And see its effect on numbers deceased,
It seems that we ought to take note of this song,
And redress the balance of what's right and what's wrong,
If death is the strength, of nuclear might,
Then hanging for murder is logically right!

Silver and Gold

Written: 1984

Love and devotion,
The seeds of a notion,
That two can live as one,
Things shared together,
Regardless of whether,
It's right at the time they are done.

The special relations,
The glanced salutations,
A message that eyes can convey.
The depth of such feeling,
In no way revealing
To others, the words it might say.

Combining their seed,
For nature to feed,
The zenith of each coupled pair,
The glory of earth,
The wonder of birth,
New generations to bear.

From struggle and strife,
The triumph of life,
A babe for the future to test.
Time lapses bold,
Parents grow old,
Offspring flee from the nest.

Surroundings look hazy,
Footsteps grow lazy,
Thoughts drift to memories past,
But nature's reminder,
Of age is much kinder,
The bond of their roots grown to last

A resurgence of pride,
Too grand to hide
New treasure and fortune untold,
Spirits arise,
Heads point to the skies,
New lives for others unfold.

The silver and gold,
Of life's cycle is told
A story as ageless as space,
But, love without end,
Should be the blend,
To flavour the whole human race

Silver Jubilation

Written: March 1986

Thank you for the invitation,
What a day to celebrate!
A silver wedding congregation,
Gathered on this special date.

Five and twenty years of sharing,
Ups and downs, you made your way,
Evidenced by love and caring,
Hallmarks of your wedding day.

Other jewels, a priceless treasure,
Gifts of life, in union blessed;
You raised and loved them without measure,
Preparing them to face life's test.

So we mark this special meeting,
Friends and loved ones young and old,
A prayer together in God's keeping,
That your silver turns to gold.

The Alarm Cock

(Why does the cock crow first thing in the morning?)

Written: 1989

This poem was made into an animated film by Cell Animation Film Co. It received a second viewing at the Cannes Film Festival 1989 in the short film section.

Some call me a rooster, some call me a cock,
I gained my spurs as a farmyard clock,
Fluffing up my feathered chest, strutting through my pen,
I cast my eye and cock my comb at any sleeping hen.
A gurgling cluck, a pause, a scratch, I stand there on one leg
I give a dig to those that may be sitting on an egg,
But every day there's one or two that turn my dewlaps red,
Refusing every move to shift them from their bed,
But, to their surprise, I've found a way to stop 'em laying late,
I launch myself upon 'em from my favourite five-barred gate,
The impact is quite stunning to the unenlightened riser,
Eyes pop out and up she runs with me perched up behind her,
So! In the early morning, and you may not think it true,
My alarming notes of triumph are your cock-a-doodle-do!

The Light Ahead

Written: February 1987

In sight of God you took your vows,
To each you pledged your troth,
Joining hands, the ring was placed,
With blessings on you both.

But after this your wedded bliss,
Depends on each of you,
Ne'er let the sun set on your wroth,
To each your word be true.

The Weather Cock

(A Bird for All Seasons)

Written: November 1986

It was not my desire, to be stuck on a spire,
For this you would think I had sinned,
A permanent perch, attached to the church,
In silent response to the wind.

For obvious reasons, I'm a bird for all seasons,
Withstanding the heat and the cold,
Cut out for all weathers, iron lungs and tin feathers,
And a glittering topcoat of gold.

Those two-timing people put me on a steeple,
My life an intolerable hell,
I can't make a sound, like those cocks on the ground,
I'm bound to the sound of a bell.

Alone in the sky, I'm a bird that can't fly,
Yet my presence can cause quite a rumpus,
When pigeon or sparrow, get lanced by my arrow,
Or land on the points of my compass.

It near' makes me cry, when a spit in the eye,
Develops to torrents of rain,
I think I've been cursed, when thunderclouds burst,
And lightning strikes for my pain!

Skies turn to blue, the sunshine breaks through,
With houses and fields spread for miles,
Up here from my seat, I see dogs in the street,
And cats chasing birds on the tiles.

Each now and then, I catch sight of a hen,
I turn purple and spin on the spot,
My efforts in vain, smoke pours from my brain,
And the balls in my bearings are shot.

It's fruitless indeed; I'm a cock that can't breed,
My parts only ravaged by time,
And the man they call Jack, who mends the odd crack,
You'd think he'd committed a crime.

The end of my plight, was on Bonfire night,
With starbursts and rockets I'm struck,
Those folks have no shame; they grin and take aim,
And think that I'm some sitting duck!

With amazing grace, I was launched into space,
I'm an orbital cock, as you'll see,
With your aerial dish, I now have my wish,
Making weather reports on TV!

Togetherness

Written: February 1987

Unspoken words, a meaningful silence,
mutually shared and satisfied by the
presence of each other; accompanied by a
glance, a smile, in reciprocal approval
of each just being there!

Vulcan QRA

(Quick Reaction Alert)

Written: December 1986

Four Vulcan aircraft on QRA readiness

Alert and reactive, response in a flash!
Second by second each one makes its dash.
Like bats out of hell, with radar eyes,
They roar down the runway and take to the skies,
The glow from their engines fade in the gloom
Delta wings cast silhouettes on the moon
Thundering on as dusk turns to night,
Throttles wide open they're soon out of sight,
Each crew their bearings, no fuss and no flap!
Each with their target, a dot on the map!

Geoff Davies, author of this book, was a Chief Technician (AFE) in the Royal Air Force – he retired from the service in 1976. Earlier in his career – between 1961 and 1965 – he flew on Lone Ranger exercises as crew member number seven with 27, 83 and 617 Vulcan Bomber Squadrons out of RAF Scampton.

In 1964, Geoff was involved in a crash-landing incident on-board Vulcan XJ824, in which the nose leg failed to lock down on the approach to Goose Bay, Labrador. About the incident, he says: 'The skipper, Flight Lieutenant Gowers, was magnificent. He landed the aircraft in dubious flying conditions – snow everywhere – without a canopy and in an air temperature of minus twenty degrees Celsius. What an experience!'

Vulcan XJ824 is currently on static display at the Imperial War Museum Duxford.

Vulcan mass display line-up

Tomorrow Never Comes

Written: May 1989

The importance of today is a memory of tomorrow,
Dulled by time, but ever there.
Day by day I stand in that square,
She died as life begun, not for me just anyone,
But here, looking back each year,
I see her as though it was only yesterday,
She hasn't gone, not really.
The rest of the day is empty, forgotten.
Tomorrow, she may be there,
Tomorrow, in that square,
Tomorrow's tomorrow, like yesterday my dear!

When I'm Calling You

(A Nurses Dilemma)

Written: April 1984

'Hello?'

'Hello!'

'Now don't you forget I'm on my own, and you have Mum don't you see,
And when disappointments like this come
along, it's very upsetting for me,
To sit by myself with no one to hear, or share in my stress or my strain,
To give you a call on my money and time, is one way of easing my brain!'

'I'm sorry dear!
I can understand that your desire for a chat,
Makes your days end a little bit better,
And a talk on the phone, brings you closer to home,
Than a few words contained in a letter.'

'Oh bother!
There it goes, and I've run out of change, and
those pips are becoming a bore,
And there's someone outside keeps shuffling
around and occasionally kicking the door.
Goodnight and take care to both you and Mum
– meantime I will beg steal or borrow,
From Tina or Helen or Matthew some coins,
to give you a phone call tomorrow!

'BYE!'

'BYE!'

From: Group Captain E S Chandler AFC RAF

Royal Air Force
Honington
Bury St Edmunds
Suffolk IP31 IEE

Honington 561 Ext 201

HON/634/8/P1

15 June 1974

Chief Technician G C A E Davies
Electrical Engineering Squadron

Dear Chief Technician Davies

I am delighted to be able to tell you that you have been awarded the Air Officer Commanding No 1 Group's Commendation in the Birthday Honours List.

This award reflects great credit upon you - many congratulations and best wishes for the future.

Yours sincerely

E. S. Chandler

Queens Birthday Honours List letter of commendation

RAF HONINGTON ELEC ENG SQN.

Come Blow Your Horn | Death Before Dishonour

To Our Faithful & Dearly Beloved
Geoffrey Charles Davies.
These Presents

Geoff, in the time we have known you, we have taken you to Our Hearts. You arrived here at Honington in 1971 to become Bay Manager of the Air Elec Bay. You have worked hard and often long hours with characteristic meticulousness and were rewarded with a well deserved AOC's Commendation. Your hobby and passion both in the RAF and the local community has been Brass Bands and your talent with the trumpet and cornet has been much sought after. You've played with the Station, British Legion, Gislingham and Newmarket Bands and it seems that no Remembrance Sunday was complete without your personal rendering of 'The Last Post'. You once played solo in front of the assembled Squadron as they sat down for dinner at the Summer Ball. Maybe it was the way we tackled the starter of corn on the cob that made you choose the tune, 'Amazing Grace.'

Well Geoff, Honington is your "Last Post" as you leave the Service after 22 years, to take a job at the local firm of 'Vintens'. We'll miss you zooming around on your 3rd hand moped and we are sure you'll miss us. Your success is assured if you tackle the job with the enthusiasm and coolness under pressure you've shown here. That coolness was shown when you were in the 'wheels-up' Vulcan at Goose Bay. You remained calm while the other Crew Chief nearly had a seizure. It was noted however that you didn't remove your bicycle clips.

So, to mark your departure, We, the Elders of Tribe, by the Powers invested in us, inaugurate you as a Full Member of the Triple-Tonguing Trumpeters. When meeting any of the undersigned members, they will greet you thus:- "How's your Trumpet Geoff?" You must then display your polished horn and demonstrate your skill with a good blow-job. Then, just like the Pied Piper lead us up to the Bar and get them in.

Remember, don't take the 'Mick' out of our Naval colleagues, after all it was a matelot who invented the lavatory seat. Admittedly it took an Airman to design the hole in it but give credit where it's due.

Given under this Seal and witnessed hereunder on the 6th August in the Year of Our Lord 1976.

A retirement tribute from the Electrical Engineering Squadron at RAF Honington

THE INSTITUTE OF SUPERVISORY MANAGEMENT

This is to certify that

GEOFFREY CHARLES DAVIES M. I. S. M.

was admitted into membership of the
Institute of Supervisory Management on the first day of

JULY 1976

Given under the common seal of the
Institute of Supervisory Management

Chairman of Council

Chairman of Membership Committee

Secretary 33025

Membership document of the Institute of Supervisory Management

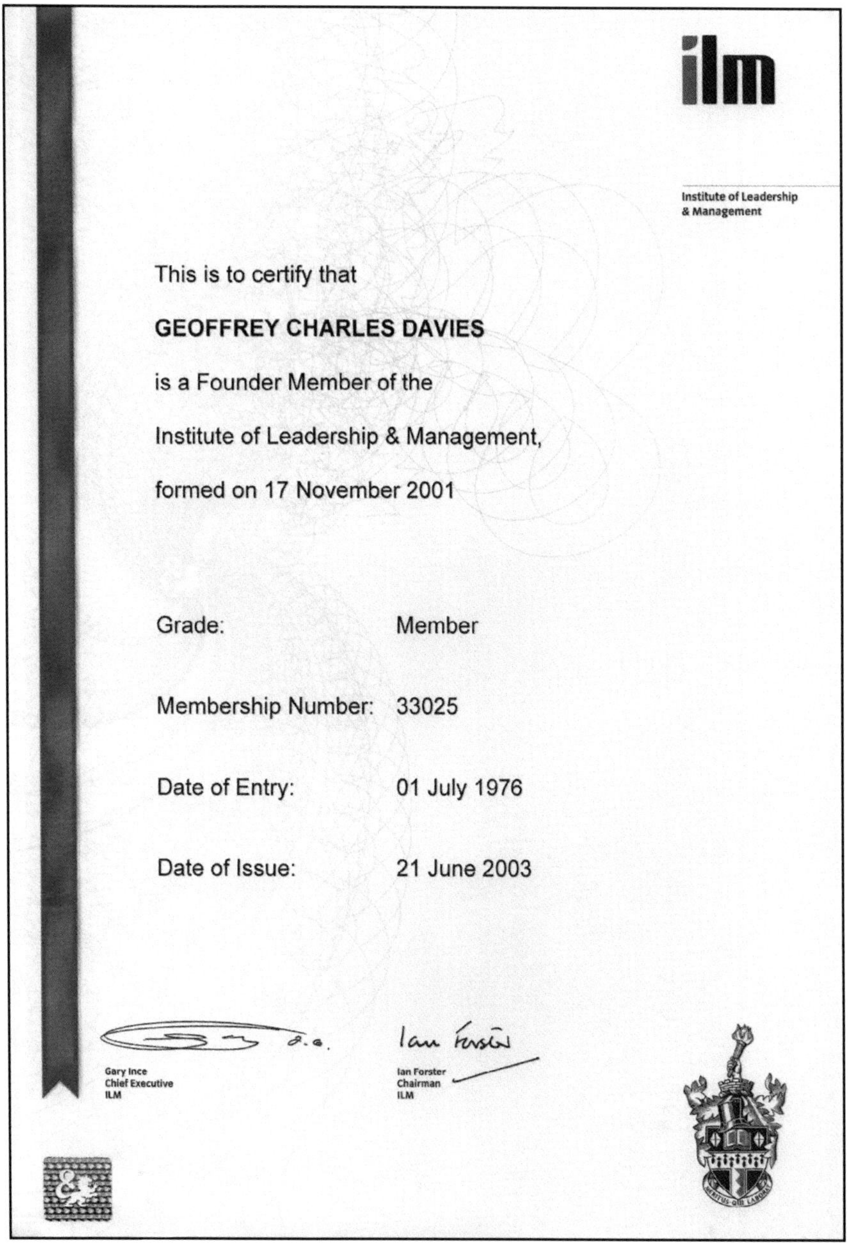

ilm

Institute of Leadership & Management

This is to certify that

GEOFFREY CHARLES DAVIES

is a Founder Member of the

Institute of Leadership & Management,

formed on 17 November 2001

Grade:	Member
Membership Number:	33025
Date of Entry:	01 July 1976
Date of Issue:	21 June 2003

Gary Ince
Chief Executive
ILM

Ian Forster
Chairman
ILM

Founder Membership document of the Institute of Leadership and Management

About Geoffrey Davies, MISM MInstLM

In the post-war years, after a brief period as a forestry student, Geoffrey Davies joined the RAF. Then, happily married with two lovely children, the family settled in West Suffolk. In 1976 Geoffrey retired from the RAF and, through a musical connection with the Royal British Legion, joined W. Vinten Ltd in Bury St. Edmunds; after a short while, he became their assistant sales and service manager in the field of aerial reconnaissance and the motion picture industry. Finally, from the beautiful county of Suffolk, Geoffrey worked as an electronic engineer for the motion picture industry, with connections in London, Chicago and Los Angeles.

Printed in Great Britain
by Amazon

22324532R00039